Southern Illinois Coal

Southern Illinois Coal
A Portfolio

C. William Horrell

Foreword by Jeffrey L. Horrell

Edited with an Introduction by Herbert K. Russell

Southern Illinois University Press
Carbondale and Edwardsville

Publication of this work was made possible in part throughthe generous
support of the Southern Illinois University Coal Extraction and Utilization
Research Center and the Southern Illinois University Foundation.

Library of Congress Cataloging-in-Publication Data

Horrel, C. William.
    Southern Illinois Coal: a portfolio / C. William Horrell; with
a foreword by Jeffrey L. Horrell; edited with an introduction
by Herbert K. Russell.
        p. cm.—(Shawnee books)

    1. Coal miners—Illinois—Pictorial works. 2. Coal miners—
Illinois —History—20th century. 3. Coal mines and mining—
Illinois—Pictorial works. 4. Coal mines and mining—Illinois—
History—20th century. I. Russell, Herbert K., 1943–II. Title.
HD8039.M6152U645 1995
305.9'622—dc20   94-13871
ISBN 0-8093-1341-3   CIP

Frontispiece: Black-faced miner. 1967.

It's dark as a dungeon and damp as the dew,

Where the danger is double and the pleasures are few,

Where the rain never falls and the sun never shines,

It's dark as a dungeon way down in the mines.

"Dark as a Dungeon"

Merle Travis

Contents

Foreword by Jeffrey L. Horrell, *ix*

Introduction by Herbert K. Russell, *xiii*

Portraits in Black and White, *1*

Deep Mines, *15*

Low Coal, *33*

Life on Top, *45*

Surface Mining, *61*

Afterwards, *83*

Foreword

Jeffrey L. Horrell

"Photography for me started in June 1936 when my mother gave me a twelve dollar folding Kodak 120 for graduation from high school. I used the kitchen sink to wash the prints and laid them out on a towel to dry."

THIS QUOTE, from unpublished notes of my father, C. William Horrell (1918–1989), describes the beginning of a career in photography lasting over fifty years. Although the equipment and printing methods changed, my father's passion for the medium was constant.

The corpus of images represented in this book constitutes several decades of documentation by Horrell of abandoned coal mines, surface and underground mines, and various aspects of the miners' lives and communities in southern Illinois. The introduction by Herbert K. Russell describes the history and context of the images. The photographs are a moment in time of a profession and community that is rapidly changing and in many instances already gone. The genesis of the project for Horrell stemmed from an interest in the unique problems encountered in coal mining and the dangers faced every day by miners. This specific interest was combined with a sense of wanting to record and preserve visually aspects of the culture and heritage of southern Illinois that were disappearing.

Horrell was born in Anna, Illinois, about twenty miles from where he spent his entire professional career. He received his undergraduate degree from Southern Illinois University (SIU) at Carbondale in 1942. During his student days, he established the first photographic services unit at SIU and was the student director until his graduation. Subsequently, he earned a master's degree from the University of Illinois (1949) and a doctorate in education from Indiana University (1955).

Interest in documentary photography for Horrell began early in his career, which centered around a photographic studio in Anna, Illinois, in the 1940s. In addition to the standard portrait work of his commercial studio, Horrell often explored and photographed the local area. An example is the picture of the "crusher man" at the Anna stone quarry in 1940, which is reproduced in *A Southern Illinois Album: Farm Security Administration Photographs, 1936–1943.*[1]

Although there was no known formal or personal connection between Horrell and photographers associated with the Farm Security Administration (FSA) project in the late 1930s and early 1940s, there certainly were parallels in their interests. Horrell, in his early career, may not have been aware of the photographs made by Arthur Rothstein of miners and mining communities of West Frankfort, Johnston City, and Carterville. However, there is no doubt of

C. William Horrell's first important mining photograph, of a "crusher man" at the Anna stone quarry. Taken in 1940, the picture is now part of the nation's most important photo collection of the Great Depression, that of the Farm Security Administration.

Horrell's understanding and appreciation of Rothstein and other FSA photographers in succeeding years.

After serving in World War II as a scriptwriter in the training film preparation unit at Scott Air Force Base, Horrell and his wife, Ettelye, returned to Anna to raise their first son, Bruce, and subsequently to open and operate the Horrell Studio. This commercial endeavor provided a wide range of experience in portrait photography as well as further opportunities for documenting the landscape and life of southern Illinois.

Horrell's career as an educator began in 1949 at Southern Illinois University at Carbondale. He was instrumental in establishing the Department of Cinema and Photography. He taught courses in photojournalism, portraiture, scientific and documentary photography, and comparative literature and photography. Horrell's teaching career spanned more than three and a half decades. His interest and enthusiasm earned him in 1971 the Excellence in Teaching Award given by SIU's College of Communications and Fine Arts. Active in professional associations related to photography, he received the Photographic Craftsman Award from the Professional Photographers of America in 1982. In collaboration with Robert A. Steffes, of California State University at Long Beach, Horrell wrote *Introductory and Publications Photography*, a textbook widely used in the United States. He also produced *A Survey of Photographic Education in the United States and Canada*, which was updated a number of times between 1969 and 1980 and published by Eastman Kodak.

Through the course of his career, Horrell made thousands of negatives but saved only about ten thousand. He preferred working in black and white for the stability and clarity of images but experimented with various color films when making several European trips. Some of his strongest work in color is of the former Yugoslavia made in the early 1980s. Horrell used successive models of Nikon cameras and lenses throughout his career and printed virtually all of his own negatives. Morris Library at Southern Illinois University at Carbondale is the repository of many of these negatives.

In the mid-1960s, Horrell became interested in social documentaries after studying and looking at works of the Farm Security Administration project as background for his teaching. He felt there was little documentation of society's everyday life, particularly in southern Illinois, and an overemphasis on the unusual and news events of the day. Shortly thereafter he offered a course in documentary photography. He patterned it after the methodology of the FSA. The course was designed with two projects—one individual and the other a group project. The former was a personal documentary in which the student would depict some aspect of present-day society that might change or disappear from the visual environment. Examples included grain silos, filling stations, railway stations, and cemeteries. The group project was the photographing of a particular community. Students selected a particular aspect of the community to photograph as a social document. Individual topics were schools, churches, diners, industries, people in various age groups, taverns or bars, and so forth. As part of the project a person from the community was invited to talk with the students about the community, its history, people, organizations, ethnic groups, problems, accomplishments, and future. At the conclusion of the project, selected photographs taken by the students were exhibited in the communities in question so people could see themselves and their communities as seen and visually interpreted by the student photographers. Many communities were documented: Anna, New Athens, Cobden, West Frankfort, Du Quoin, and Pinckneyville. The University Archives at Southern Illinois University at Carbondale and the Illinois State Archives include these collections among their holdings.

It was through his interest in social documentary, as noted in his teaching, that in 1966 Horrell began a comprehensive documentary of southern Illinois that resulted in the pictures for *Land Between the Rivers: The Southern Illinois Country*.[2] As part of his photographic exploration for the book, he began photographing coal mines, miners, and their communities. The "Black-faced miner" of 1967 serves as the frontispiece of this book and has been reproduced many times. The image of the miner with his face blackened by coal dust, and details such as the "Union Made" snaps of his overalls, exemplify the strength and dignity that Horrell attempted to capture in his portraits of miners.

From the end of the 1960s through the mid-1980s, Horrell continued his work on coal mining. In the late 1970s, a traveling exhibition entitled "Images of Coal" consisting of Horrell's photographs was organized. The exhibit depicted different aspects of the coal mining industry in southern Illinois, including portraits, mining equipment, and the mines themselves. Some of the photographs in this book were exhibited in that show.

In describing his own work and techniques in an interview, Horrell said: "I express what I think is important. Photography is my means of communicating. I am a straight photographer. I don't understand photographs that are ultramanipulated. Hopefully, my photographs will give the viewer some useful information and enjoyment."[3]

This is a collective portrait of an industry, a way of life, and the people associated with it. Horrell cared deeply about the hardworking individuals and their livelihoods in the coal communities of southern Illinois, and it was his hope that these images would preserve their heritage for all of us.

Notes

1. Herbert K. Russell, with a Foreword by F. Jack Hurley, *A Southern Illinois Album: Farm Security Administration Photographs, 1936–1943* (Carbondale: Southern Illinois University Press, 1990), p. 58.

2. C. William Horrell, Henry Dan Piper, and John W. Voigt, *Land Between the Rivers: The Southern Illinois Country* (Carbondale: Southern Illinois University Press, 1973).

3. Ruth Strack, "SIU-C Photo Expert 'Doc' Horrell Retiring," *Southern Illinoisan*, June 22, 1983, Franklin Today Section, p. 1.

Introduction

Herbert K. Russell

C. William Horrell was something of a rarity in academic circles. An excellent photographer who had had his own studio and enjoyed a fine record for placing his pictures in top publications, Horrell served for thirty-four years at Southern Illinois University (SIU) before retiring as a professor in the Department of Cinema and Photography in 1983. But none of Horrell's degrees was in photography. Indeed, his bachelor's in sociology and master's and doctorate in education sometimes suggested he had prepared for disciplines other than the one for which he is remembered. The chief reason for this is that few colleges or universities offered the photography programs Horrell wanted or needed as he progressed in knowledge and degrees. A related fact is that this didn't matter; much of his success was the result of lifelong education outside the classroom.

A most important component of this education was the hand-held camera his mother gave him in 1936 when he was eighteen. This not only provided his first sense of what he might record photographically but also led him to an understanding of the chemical requirements of film: when he decided that film processing costs were too expensive, he purchased a basic film developing kit and began doing his own work. His WWII experiences as a scriptwriter for Army training films complemented his personal interests, and at war's end he opened his own studio in his hometown of Anna and managed it for four years before becoming director of Southern Illinois University's Photographic Services in 1949.

Concurrent with these activities was the refinement and popular acceptance of what was to be the chief artistic influence on Horrell's career, "documentary photography." This kind of photography emphasizes true-to-life situations while ignoring cosmetic enhancements in favor of a realism so unambiguous that captions are sometimes superfluous. By the time Horrell arrived at SIU, documentary photography had already found its first important national application during the years 1935–43 as a part of President Franklin Roosevelt's Farm Security Administration (FSA). Photographers working for the FSA had taken pictures that were simultaneously so bleak and stunning that they not only helped win approval for FDR's social programs but also left a permanent pictorial record of America during the Great Depression. Horrell greatly admired the work of the FSA photographers. He incorporated their techniques into the courses he taught and eventually applied them to his own work.

A major irony of Horrell's career is that two of his own early pictures were a part of the FSA collection, but he was unaware of this until shortly before his death. In the early 1940s, Horrell had been a student at Southern Illinois University where one of his professors admired two of his pictures and sent them to the Farm Security Administration in Washington, D.C. The FSA had some of the finest photographers in the nation (Walker Evans, Dorothea Lange, Marion Post Wolcott, Arthur Rothstein, and others), and the odds of Horrell's pictures being accepted were rather small. But his pictures were accepted. Unfortunately, because the FSA operated with only a skeleton staff and on a shoestring budget, Horrell did not learn that his pictures had been made a part of the FSA collection until 1988 when an acquaintance informed him of it. The news was a happy conclusion to Horrell's long love affair with photography: he was a part of an important national collection that he had admired for much of his professional career.

During his lifetime, Horrell's photographs routinely appeared in a wide variety of major metropolitan newspapers, including the *Baltimore Sun*, *Indianapolis Star*, *St. Louis Post-Dispatch*, *St. Louis Globe-Democrat*, *Chicago Tribune*, and others. He also published his pictures in a host of popular and specialty magazines, including *Life*, *Pic*, *Youth*, *Friends*, and others. This wide range of publications notwithstanding, most southern Illinoisans were unaware of Horrell's pictorial record, not only because credits for his pictures were not always printed with his work but also because he distributed and sold many of his pictures through a third party in New York, the Black Star agency.

In 1973, Horrell's acceptance in southern Illinois changed dramatically when he provided photographs for the most successful pictorial history of the region, *Land Between the Rivers*. Horrell suddenly found himself famous (or reasonably so) in an area he knew and loved. He was called upon to speak at cultural gatherings, heard his pictures described as art, and found himself the subject of one-man shows, including pictures on permanent display at Southern Illinois University's Coal Research Center.

The latter was a particularly apt setting, for Horrell's coal mining pictures are the best since Franklin Roosevelt's FSA photographer Arthur Rothstein visited southern Illinois during the Great Depression. Like Rothstein, Horrell was interested in all aspects of coal's extraction as well as its sociology, for example, company-owned towns, houses, and schools. Unlike Rothstein, Horrell was able to gain admission to certain underground mines in which truly adverse mining conditions existed—those shown herein as "low coal mines."

Low coal or "scratchback" mines are known by a number of names (including "thin coal" or "crawl" mines) but are alike in that they offer the most challenging and claustrophobic of mining environments: they are all too low for a miner to stand upright. The terms "five-foot coal" or (worse) "four-foot coal" describe both the vertical height of the coal seam as well as the vertical height of the area in which the miners are working. The miners may work close to the mine entryway or travel horizontally underground for several miles before they begin their tasks. Several of Horrell's pictures show men working under these conditions. The pictures were probably taken in the Harrisburg-McLeansboro area where low coal is relatively common.

Most of Horrell's pictures were taken in mines more typical of southern Illinois, where coal seams average six to eight feet in height. Horrell's pictures show a wide variety of occupations and machinery, but the machine that was dominating underground mines (or "deep" mines) in 1966 (when Horrell first visited the mines) was the so-called continuous miner. It not only changed the methods of coal's extraction but also left a photographer with an entirely new set of images to consider.

The continuous miner virtually eliminated the time-honored four-step process of mining coal. This involved cutting or picking the coal loose at the bottom of a seam and then drilling holes and blasting (with compressed air or explosives) before loading the loosened coal into a coal car. The continuous miner merged these four steps into one: a broad drum with carbide-tipped teeth now ripped the coal from the seam and passed it along a conveyer past the operator and into a waiting shuttle car (or "coal buggy"); the coal buggy then carried the coal to a coal car or a moving conveyer belt, which carried the coal out of the mine.

The advent of the continuous miner changed the daily life of thousands of miners by largely eliminating two of the most dangerous practices of traditional mining: blasting, and making the "cut" along the base of a coal seam before blasting. The cut caused the loosened coal to fall at the bottom of the seam instead of being hurled back at the miners or otherwise scattered about by the blast. Unfortunately, blasting with explosives was an inexact science that could bring down the roof as well as loosening the coal and was especially controversial when it involved "shooting on shift"—was carried out while the mine was full of workers other than blasters. The continuous miner also eliminated many jobs outright. There is not one picture of a miner with a pick and shovel among Horrell's many photographs, nor are there any prints of miners loading coal by hand.

Even the folklore of mines was changed by this new mechanization. A decade before Horrell entered the mines, the popular song "Sixteen Tons" had described a miner from the old days who worked all day to hand load sixteen tons of coal into an underground coal car. (This was, by the way, three or four times the amount that an average miner might actually mine on an average shift.) The tune reached the top of the American song charts and stayed there for weeks, in part because of the haunting question of the song's refrain: "You load sixteen tons and what do you get?"

In contrast, the miners in Horrell's photos knew exactly what they would get: they would receive about $7,500 per year if they were working in the mid-1960s, or double that in the mid-70s —provided, of course, that their machines didn't dig more coal than industry could use, and that their unions didn't go out on strike. As for laboring all day to load sixteen tons, well, that too was a thing of the past. Even a small continuous miner could mine and load four tons of coal per minute (by the 1990s, more sophisticated models would mine nearly four times that). Horrell had caught the southern Illinois coal industry at a pivotal place in its development: the old days of sixteen tons per day were soon to be replaced by sixteen tons per minute. The industry was more economical, cleaner, and safer than it had ever been.

Two of these safety techniques show up repeatedly in Horrell's pictures, and because each of them favorably influenced the quality of his pictures, it will be useful to comment on them. By the late 1960s, a major cause of mine disasters in the past—explosions and fires fueled by airborne coal dust—had largely been eliminated. Through the 1930s, for example, many Illinois mines had suspended crushed limestone from mine roofs in such a way that an explosion might send the rock dust cascading to the floor—thus extinguishing the fire that often followed a split second later. By Horrell's time, however, it was common to rock dust the floor of the mine as well as its sides (or "ribs") and roof (or "top") immediately after mining. It is this limestone dust that lends a chalky white appearance to many of Horrell's underground pictures. It also has the unintended effect of creating more informative pictures since the whiteness of the limestone reflects the light and provides more details than might otherwise be seen.

The industry's modern means of supporting the tops of mines also had a beneficial effect on Horrell's pictures. There are very few mine timbers, posts, or wooden "cribs" supporting mine ceilings and obscuring one's view (and getting in the way of machinery) because the tops of most of these mines are supported by roof bolts. These are three-to-ten-foot-long bolts that are machine-driven into holes drilled into the roof. As the bolt's final turns are administered, its top end expands, and a self-contained, quick-drying glue seals the bolt in place. A heavy block of wood or metal flange is then fitted onto the exposed end of the bolt and fastened in place. The strength of the roof bolts is suggested by the fact that the average coal mine in southern Illinois is about 650 feet deep; it is this overhead mass that the roof bolts are stabilizing. Roof bolts show up in the tops of many of Horrell's pictures, often under a heavy talcum of rock dust. Even with the addition of roof bolts, however, it is not uncommon for a mine to experience roof falls.

The most likely area for a fall to occur is near the "face," the area in which coal is being mined. A working face is simultaneously the most fascinating and enigmatic part of a mine, not only because one is disturbing what has been in place for about 300 million years (the coal), but also because it is here that the business of mining is carried on amid a backdrop of noise, dust, and semidarkness.

A mine may have any number of faces and workers. The usual crew at a given face consists of the operator of a continuous miner and a helper, two or three shuttle car operators, and a utility person. A roof bolting team and repair personnel will also be nearby.

Any number of things can bring mining to a halt. If the face boss or mine supervisor (or a mine inspector) discovers "bad top," additional roof bolts will have to be added before mining can continue (only the cutting drum of the continuous miner extends beyond the last roof bolt; the operator remains on the safe side). Or a water problem may slow work on a face. Mines pass under rivers, creeks, and lakes, and miners routinely encounter wet conditions that require pumping millions of gallons of water. Inadequate airflow or elevated levels of explosive methane gas (alias "firedamp") may also halt mining.

Or perhaps the surveyors are working near a face. It is necessary to know exactly where one is in an underground mine, not only to avoid trespassing on the coal rights of others but also to avoid breaking into old mines filled with gas or water. Underground surveying is also necessary to avoid cutting into oil or gas wells, and to observe the demands of a popular form of coal extraction known as "room and pillar" mining. After the surveyors have done their work, the top of the mine is marked with a directional line for the operator of the continuous miner to follow.

Horrell recorded all of these phenomena, often showing a particular interest in the various types of haulage vehicles. Powered by batteries or electric power cables, the largest of these shuttle cars nearly fill mine passageways from top to bottom and side to side. The largest haulage vehicles are seldom turned around after they enter the confines of a mine. Instead, after a driver arrives at his destination, he moves to a seat opposite the one he has been occupying and drives back in the direction he came by using a second set of foot controls and a side-mounted steerage system. Horrell shows these massive machines squeezing down narrow passageways with inches to spare as they carry the coal from the face to the conveyer belts.

He also photographed much larger vehicles, most notably those in several southern Illinois surface (or "strip") mines. Some of the largest self-propelled vehicles in the world have figured in these. Horrell's pictures of the stripping shovel called *The Captain* (or Marion 6360) are illustrative. Used to remove the dirt and rock (or "overburden") above a coal seam, *The Captain* stood 25 stories tall and weighed 29 million pounds. It was so big that its crew went to their work stations via an elevator rather than a stairway. The crawlers propelling it were similar to those used by NASA to move missiles onto the launching pad at the Kennedy Space Center.

Horrell's surface mining pictures also serve to destroy a stereotype regarding surface mining, namely the misconception that such mining leaves properties as permanent wastelands. Horrell photographed numerous mined sites that had been reclaimed to yield parks, orchards, hayfields, pastures, and field crops. Some coal companies operating in southern Illinois had practiced such procedures years before a 1977 federal law mandated such practices. But many had not, and Horrell took pictures showing the results of both methods.

In addition to showing the scale of surface mining machines and their impact on the land, Horrell also took numerous pictures showing the techniques of surface mining. This

usually begins with a bulldozer to clear the area and partially level it. Holes are then drilled in the overburden and explosives inserted and set off to loosen the soil and rock. A dragline or stripping shovel then removes the overburden and places it in a "spoil pile," after which the coal is removed by smaller shovels. (This procedure was still essentially the same when this book was published, except that the topsoil and other soil strata are now stacked separately and replaced in sequence when mining is completed.)

The question of whether to surface mine a particular seam or not depends on two considerations, the depth of the coal seam and its thickness. In Illinois, it is usually not economical to surface mine coal that lies deeper than 150–200 feet. If the cost of removing the overburden and replacing it during reclamation is greater than the anticipated profits from the coal, then there is no financial incentive to mine.

Horrell was also interested in related activities of mining—in coal's processing, cleaning, and transportation (by rail and barge in particular), as well as in the daily, behind-the-scenes operations that keep mines and miners working. He took numerous photos showing maintenance and shop activities as well as above-ground matters such as mapping the layout of a mine. Horrell also highlighted the beauty of the commonplace—in the clothes of the miners, their dinner pails, and daily tools and accoutrements such as ropes and oilcans. He could show as often as he wished, apparently, that even common articles assume their own elegance when the photographer's sense of composition is correct.

The same might be said of his pictures taken after the completion of mining. Horrell shows us the weathered boards of company houses; the imposing iron beauty of an ancient tipple; the grassy sidewalks of an old coal town; an abandoned building against a lowering sky as a storm approaches. Most of these seem given to time and the elements, the activities of long ago now only a memory.

Some of the vocations and equipment Horrell photographed have largely disappeared. It is doubtful, for example, that there are many "lamp houses" remaining. These housed the safety lamps that showed the presence of gas through a change in the color of the flame (this is now accomplished electronically through much smaller devices). Nor are there as many "drillers" as there once were. In the larger mines, in particular, their work has been taken over by the continuous miner.

In some of the pictures, where a once-great machine has been abandoned to weeds and

The Captain. *A stripping shovel weighing 29 million pounds, it stood 25 stories tall and was one of the world's largest stripping shovels. Note the human figure at right. Percy.*

corrosion, there seems a terrible waste. But Horrell's captions are not judgmental, and it is often impossible to determine what he himself thought of such outcomes. In general, he followed the dicta of the documentary photographers he admired: the picture, not the caption, should do the "talking."

Horrell certainly followed this guideline in the captions he left. He supplied at least seventeen captions for pictures used in his traveling exhibit in the mid-1970s, but most of these are very brief, consisting of only three or four words and occasionally a date and place; several of these pictures and captions have been used in this book. Eight of the pictures that follow were first printed in *Land Between the Rivers*, and some captions have been derived from this source as well. Horrell also drafted typed comments for pictures for a never-to-be-completed overview of southern Illinois coal. In a few instances, Horrell left prints of the same picture with more than one caption and date. This was probably the result of his trying different development techniques on a given negative while searching for an appropriate description of the picture. Picture captions traceable to Horrell as well as those derived by editing his draft comments are shown in this book in roman type (the same in which these comments are printed). Pictures for which Horrell left no captions have been provided captions in italics. Horrell's coal mining pictures were taken throughout the southern Illinois Coal Belt across a twenty-year period from 1966 to 1986. Most were taken between 1967 and 1977.

Toward the Gulf of Mexico. Coal barges round a bend on the Mississippi. Grand Tower.

Portraits in Black and White

A mine boss.

3

Miner with an artificial hand waits for the shift to start. 1973.

Underground miner. 1967.

Before the shift.

A woman miner waits to go underground.

Woman miner at a union meeting.

Surface mine welder. 1967.

Miner at a union meeting.

11

Mine worker in a white hard hat.

Underground miner.

13

Deep Mines

Early morning shift at a very small mine.

Going underground. Saline County. 1967.

Underground entryway. Note the conveyer belt in the center along with high voltage cables and roof bolts showing heavy rock dusting.

Roof bolter.

A "mucker." The machine is driven by compressed air and is used here
to load rocks blasted loose during the sinking of a mine shaft.

Underground surveyor.

Measuring the amount of fresh air with an anemometer.

Business end of a continuous miner. Canvas curtains to the rear and right channel fresh air to the face.

Rock dusting a recently mined area. A surveyor's marker
—the string with the note attached—is visible at top left.

The Hoot Owl Express, *a shuttle car. The double seats, side-mounted steering wheel,*
and dual foot controls allow the driver to reverse direction by changing seats.

Lunchtime underground.

Controls of a boring type of continuous miner. The ducting at left delivers fresh air to the face.

A shuttle car moves through a narrow mine corridor. The chain conveyer in the foreground loads the coal as it comes from the continuous miner.

29

A miner leaves a slope mine, a mine with a sloping entryway rather than a vertical shaft.

End of the shift. Harrisburg.

Low Coal

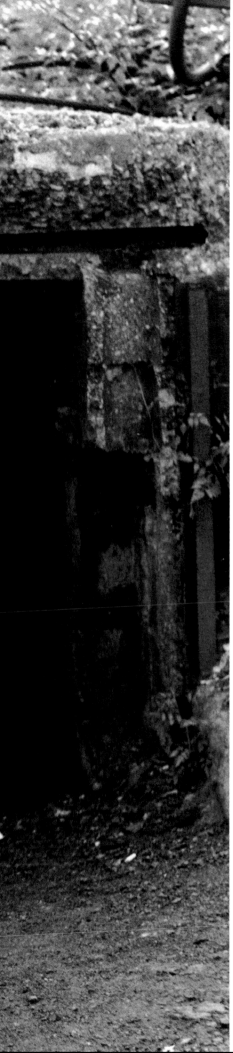

Underground mine with low entryway.

Interior of a low coal mine. The height of this mine from its floor to its roof is only four to five feet.

A mine superintendent (right) confers with a face boss in a low coal mine.

Driller in a low coal mine.

Roof bolter in a low coal mine.

Low coal machine operator.

Materials tractor and operator in a low coal mine.

Low coal mine superintendent with a sounding rod. The sound made by tapping
the rod against the roof helps in determining whether the roof is safe.

Life on Top

Lamp house at a small coal mine.

Wash room. Street clothes hang from hooks as the miners work. Work clothes
will dry there in preparation for the next day's shift. 1968.

Map of an underground coal mine showing room-and-pillar method of extraction.

A load of raw coal enters the crusher house of a small mine.

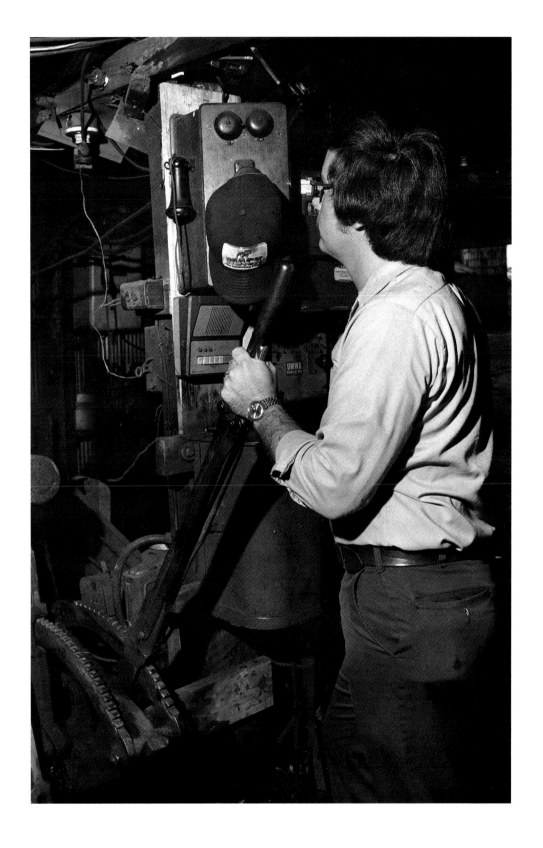

Hoisting engineer at a small mine.

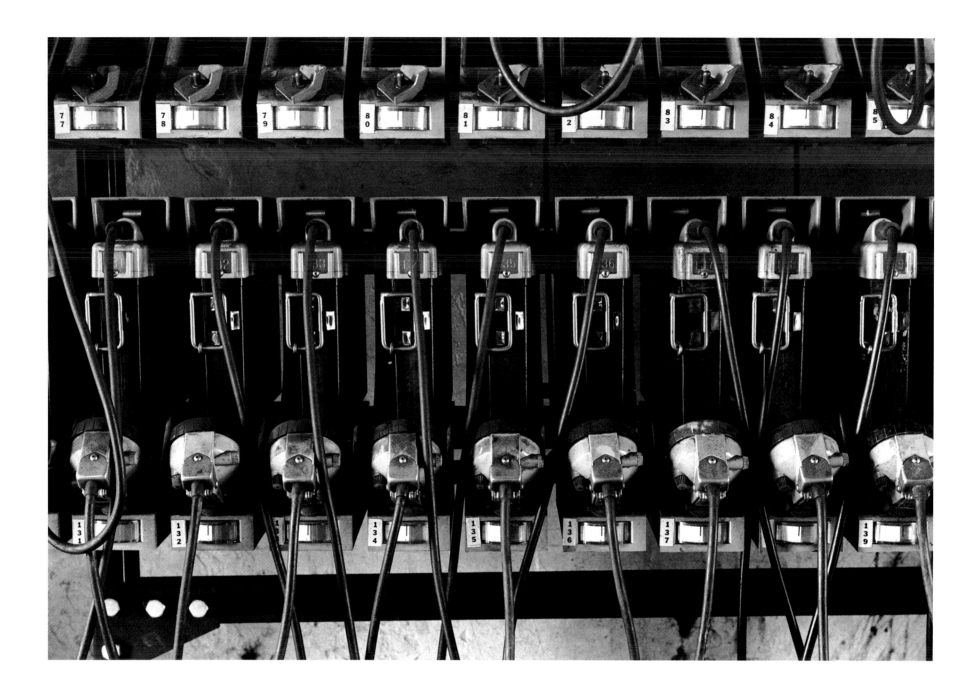

Miners' lamp batteries being recharged.

Machinist working on a mining machine.

Inside a preparation house. Coal washers separate the coal from slate, rocks, and other materials.

Piles of raw coal awaiting transfer to a preparation house.

Night construction
of a coal storage silo.

Coal car loading. 1969.

Coal loading facility at a small mine. 1967.

59

A coal train prepares to leave
southern Illinois as empties await filling.

Surface Mining

Strip shovel. 1969.

63

The *King of Spades*, a stripping shovel. Drilling rigs at the left open the ground for explosives, which break up the rock and soil above the coal.

Aerial view of a coal stripping shovel.

Boom of a
stripping shovel.

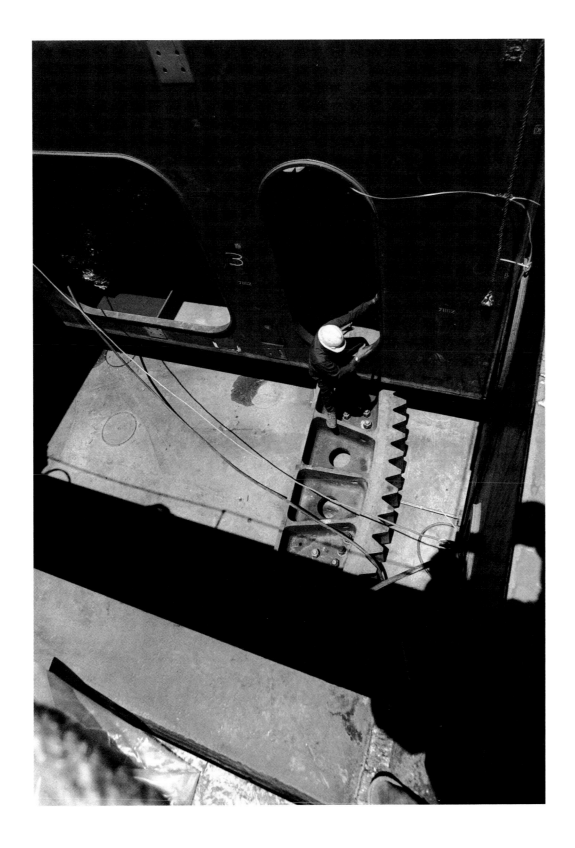

A worker moves gingerly among the enormous parts
of a dragline under construction.

A worker tightens a bolt on the interior of a dragline.

The giant treads of *The Captain*, a stripping shovel. Percy.

The Captain at lunchtime. The machine's power cable is at left. Percy.

Welding a new tooth on a bucket.

Surface mining in summary: a small shovel loads a truck while a drill bores holes for the placement of explosives. In the distance, a dragline removes loosened soil and rock to expose the coal seam.

Maintenance of a haulage vehicle at a surface mine.

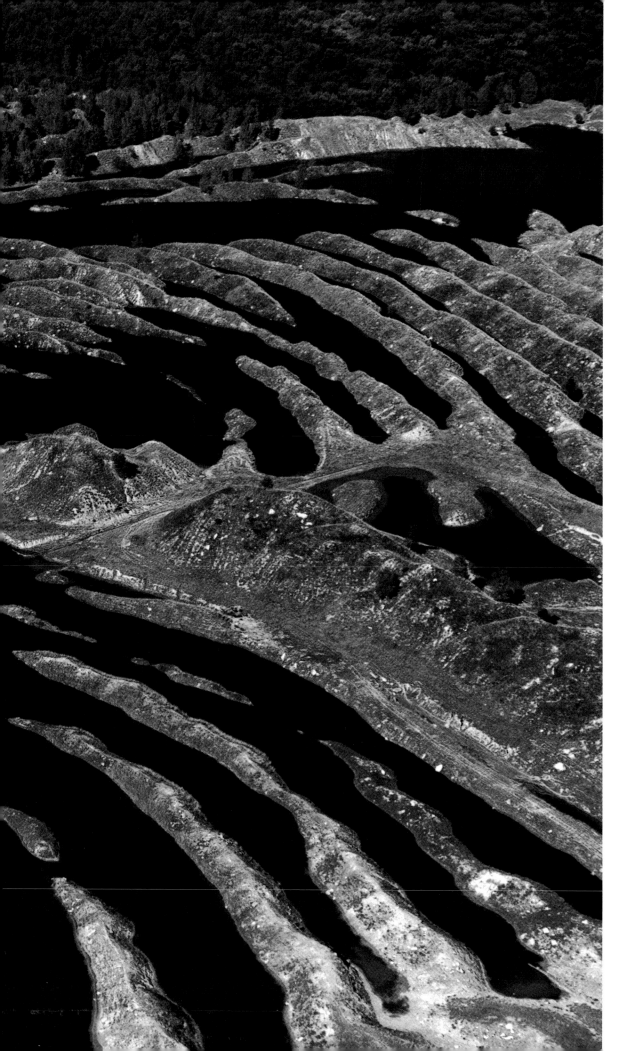

Abandoned strip mine filled with water. 1968.

A vineyard on reclaimed mine land.

Afterwards

Coal tipple of a closed mine.

83

Abandoned train loading structure. 1967.

85

Old mine shop. Royalton.

Overturned haulage car
at an abandoned mine.   89

Metal forge in an abandoned coal mine.

Abandoned stripping shovel. 1967.

Old scale house. 1977.

A small shovel being overtaken
by trees and plant growth.

93

Reinforced concrete tipple. Muddy.

A company schoolhouse.

Old company houses. Muddy.

Company house. Hallidayboro. 1975.

Union hall. Valier. 1968.

Clothing in the wash room of an abandoned mine.

JEFFREY L. HORRELL is librarian of the Fine Arts Library at Harvard University, Cambridge, Massachusetts. He is the younger son of C. William Horrell and grew up in Carbondale, Illinois. He received master's degrees in library science and in the history of art from the University of Michigan and is currently working toward a Ph.D. degree in fine arts from Syracuse University. He has held library posts at the University of Michigan, Dartmouth College, and Syracuse University. He has written in the field of art librarianship and on photography, including *Treasures of the Hood Museum of Art, Dartmouth College.*

HERBERT K. RUSSELL is director for college relations at John A. Logan College, Carterville, Illinois. A native Illinoisan, he received his Ph.D. degree in English from Southern Illinois University, where he taught the subject and subsequently served as editorial writer and technical editor at the university's Coal Research Center. He is the editor of *A Southern Illinois Album: Farm Security Administration Photographs, 1936–1943*; a new edition of Mary Tracy Earle's Civil War novel *The Flag on the Hilltop*; and a poetry anthology *The Enduring River: Edgar Lee Masters' Uncollected Spoon River Poems.*

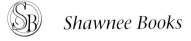 *Shawnee Books*

Also available in this series . . .

The Next New Madrid Earthquake
A Survival Guide for the Midwest
William Atkinson

Vernacular Architecture in Southern Illinois
The Ethnic Heritage
John M. Coggeshall and Jo Anne Nast

The Flag on the Hilltop
Mary Tracy Earle

A Nickel's Worth of Skim Milk
A Boy's View of the Great Depression
Robert J. Hastings

A Penny's Worth of Minced Ham
Another Look at the Great Depression
Robert J. Hastings

The Music Came First
The Memoirs of Theodore Paschedag
As Told to Thomas J. Hatton

Always of Home
A Southern Illinois Childhood
Edgar Allen Imhoff

Heartland Blacksmiths
Conversations at the Forge
Richard Reichelt

Fishing Southern Illinois
Art Reid

A Southern Illinois Album
Farm Security Administration Photographs, 1936–1943
Herbert K. Russell